Cerulean

Ahmed AboElhiba

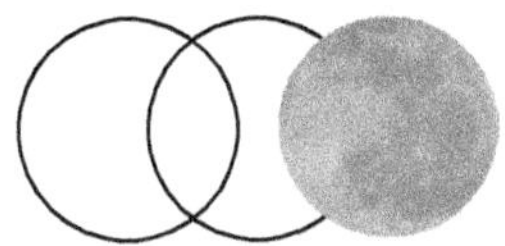

To whom has been tortured by
the imminence of endings and
goodbyes, and the fables of
forever and eternal highs.

TABLE OF CONTENTS

AHMED ABOELHIBA

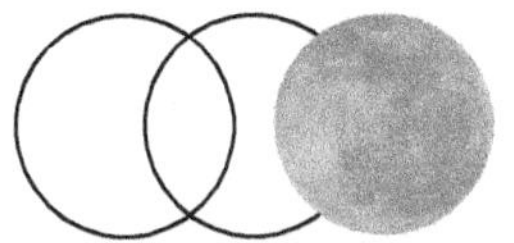

The Interlude

AHMED ABOELHIBA

At The End of The Day

At the end of the day,
I am sat alone

In an empty hall,
on the hollowness throne

Blind their eyes are,
and past me they can only see

Deaf their ears are,
and the screams of agony they
cannot hear

At the end of the day,
I realize people aren't always forever

And I shelved myself off,
a thought I assumed was clever

Robber my mind is,
stealing away any bits of peace
I get to experience

Dweller in my heart,
is an ache fuming by any minor
inconvenience

In Saltwater, I'm A Crawdad

Showed up to the party,
approaching one of tables
as I have sat alone

While everyone here has their person,
sharing moments on the dance floor

Vicariously I live through them,
and yet I wonder when will my time be

To open up a rusty valve of my heart,
one pouring love infinitely

And is it something in me I wonder,
as it's an experience I never had

Am I undeserving?
Is it not my place to be?
As if in saltwater, I'm a crawdad

And of emotions,
my heart has grown full,
ringing like an enormous bell

...

Yet of neglect,
it has shallowed from within,
aching like a hollow shell

As if there's this layer existing,
blinding their pupils from an exact,
true vision of me

As if I am just invisible,
left unseen as I tirelessly envision
who I am meant to be

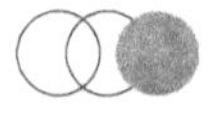

Chapter I:
Sceneries

Imminence

The insignificant silence
of passing strangers,
to the non-awkward silence
between close friends

To the festering silence
and its consequent dangers,
as it chops off a bond
that was never to end

Tireless efforts are exerted in vain,
and the sweet memories have bitterly
wilted away

All the prayers ask for heavy rain,
to brush off the heaviness that on
heart does weigh

Somehow bright hues wash out and fade;
dazzling lights dull off and do lose
their shine

Endless radiance is a pure masquerade,
delusions that cage up happiness and
confine

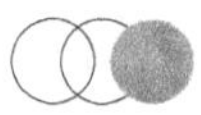

Sceneries

Haunted I am,
by perfect sceneries
I didn't capture

By chances I didn't give,
by not better appreciating
moments of rapture

Through memory,
my mind teleports me back to
the blood moon we both saw

How we followed trails
to an elite shot,
how our eyes mused with complete awe

Through time,
I vividly remember the moment I have
found in you a dear friend

How you enthused me
to articulate my thoughts,
how to create art that transcends

...

Through thoughts,
my soul drowns within seas of burden
as it revisits conversations

Fallacies in an ideal argument,
imperfections in the most endearing
situations

And I find myself tormented,
by the memories of sceneries
I frequently capture

By the chances I have given,
by looking into life with an
inconsistent aperture

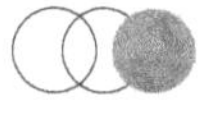

Totem

Don't you think it is
too unfair of the world,
to taunt me by you at every
possible occasion?

Details I'd never forget
of places you like,
and they conquer my mind
as a brutal invasion

Fresh-smelling atmosphere
of books,
here I am on a bench
writing a poem

Heartwarming comfort
of packed shelves,
to this place
you are the totem

Oh man, I would say it
straight to your face,
I just miss your friendship
and company

. . .

Aching I am for the times we
spent in bookstores, spending
all we had of money

Don't you think it was
too cruel of you,
to bolt away as lighting,
with no valid reason?

And couldn't you do
me a small favor by talking it out,
instead of your silent treason?

We'll Never Know

We'll never know,
how suddenly we have clicked
like perfect puzzle pieces

How our personalities overlap,
and how our commonality increases

We'll never know,
how overly supportive to each other
we supposedly are

How it is there
until I get what you don't,
how it injures you as a rooted scar

We'll never know,
how you have ordered a decree to let
go of someone who was once close

How you disregarded the car-rides
and late night talks,
and maybe your ego grew grandiose

...

We'll never know,
how our beings will navigate us when
we encounter each other once again

How we'll make sense of your contempt
flavoring a sourness,
in what would have sweet been

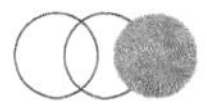

Helping Hand

Whenever I was drowning deep down,
you were the helping hand

Extending through the seas of burden,
carrying me gently to land

When the tides pull me back again,
you were the oxygen in my lungs

The sleep to an insomniac,
to a ladder of dreams you were the
rungs

As I have counted on your presence,
you have away migrated

I ran out of breath,
and midst drowning, I felt entirely
dehydrated

To aid a helpless soul,
I pulled myself off to the shore,
despite the endless tiredness

Without your oxygen or helping hand,
I did realize, by myself I acquired
this

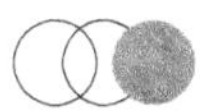

On Your Own

Grateful you once were,
to have a friend as precious as me

Someone overwhelmingly kind,
and to a secret is a trustee

Elated you once were,
by the time we have around each other
spent

Conversing in deepest thoughts;
a type of bond not bound to a descent

Enthused you once were,
to have a creative mind present
by your side

One raptured by your triumphs,
yet to your resentment it couldn't
abide

Blessed I once felt,
to almost know what it's like
to have a real friend

. . .

Yet it shattered me,
to know for sure that everything
sweet does end

Incandescent you must feel now,
to be free from the shackles of
someone tainted in shades of blue

And yet you were my ray of light,
and our friendship almost had me
remolding into a person so new

On your own you are now, bud,
and may you find solace, away from
the echoes of what has passed

Moving ahead I shall now try,
and may I throw away the grudges
we might have at one another cast

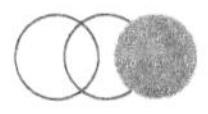

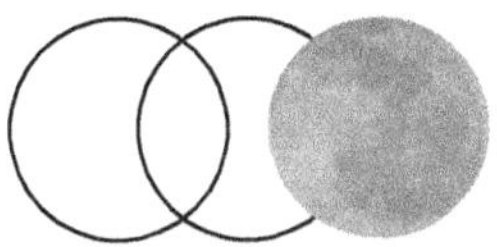

Chapter II:
Scrutiny

Archived

Crumbling and sparingly drawling,
from a cliff I was myself hauling

No distinct intentions I had,
of either life or death

Yet a deep harshness I felt,
of a suffocating breath

Blasting through my ears were give-up
chants, yet I couldn't have myself to
them abide

Thinking about those before me who
once did, I see how their vibrance
has bitterly died

Agonizing my mind is a despairing
feeling, festering by unrequited
deep emotions

Someone they can depend on, I always
am, and in return I'm left drowning
in oceans

. . .

Patching the hollowness within me
I am, with fantasies that should
be doing the job

A fake sense of validation I aim to
feel, through delusions such feelings
I get to rob

Merely I will remain,
the correct answer one realizes
after a test ends

Late of a discovery,
one left archived; one scientists
wouldn't expend

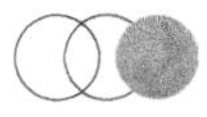

Delusions

Within every place I go,
I'm always haunted by the sneaking
shadows of what could have been

Sweet moments I would have
experienced;
eternal memories that would
have happened therein

Within every moments of sleep,
my mind reimagines realities where
I experience true company

People seeing me for who I am;
friends caring about me like I'm part
of their extended family

Within every despairing poem I write,
my muses star as main characters in a
life that was never theirs

Shades of green recolored
into grayscale;
enthusiasm they have replaced
with apathetic shares

...

Within reflective moments
I force myself into,
my mind tries to make sense of all the
tragic endings and pitiful situations

Betrayals of heart from
the closest of friends;
deep wounds they have unstitched after
the severest surgical operations

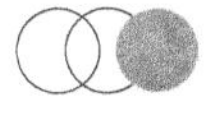

M.N.R.

Most notorious reputation I got
for seeing in people their ultimate
best

For believing in them beyond doubt,
while they for themselves try to quest

Most notorious reputation I got
for not owing people explanations

Explanations for who I am
or what I do, or why I never
disclose vacations

Most notorious reputation they got
for jumping off cliffs they cannot
survive

For ruining streaks of golden days,
and for the deepest of blues they
strive

...

Much needed rest I wish myself
from their festering toxicity that
I haven't from healed

Much needed rest I wish them
from the profound disdain that
has their hearts peeled

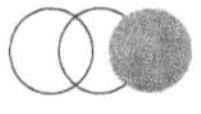

Timelines

Sometimes I think
of my childhood friends

Those I met on playgrounds;
a bond never meant to end

I recall the times
we spent together, so bright

Ten years, I assume,
worth a lifetime's delight

The cycle of life carried us away,
and has come through

A timeline that once harbored us,
eventually itself withdrew

Sometimes I wonder
who my teenage friends
have now become

We dreamt of endless futures;
I hope of such they have
achieved some

...

I wonder if by some mystical means,
our timelines would weave back in
spotless sync

A reconciliation of sweet company,
whose memories are marked with
permanent ink

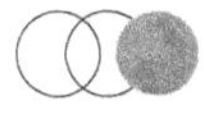

Speak Not.

From bygone wounds
I can still feel the sting,
as I hold on to moments,
in this weary plot

I see tornadoes tearing
lands of my comfort,
and about them,
I'm forced to speak not

My carefree soul,
demanded at all times,
though it withered
many years ago

An upbeat facade
veiled my hidden blues,
until it plateaued,
refusing to grow

One day I saw my spirit swallowed
whole, into a realm so dark and gray

By consequence, those who cared
found themselves in a swift getaway

A Person Misread

For the longest of times,
I assured myself they would hate me
the more they've known me

Yet, for once,
I had a feeling my complexity could be
appreciated if into me they could see

And I do not blame them for running
away, after seeing an exposure of me
they did not expect

Yet, I pray I'd find someone staying
by my side, even knowing that I'm a
human not so perfect

Through teenage years, I knew I was
not charming or endearing, even as
I've owned a heart so kind

It didn't help being a person of
intellect either, even as I have
ventured into the world with a
savvy mind

. . .

And maybe I am still young, maybe I
still got a lifetime ahead

Maybe the lone sailor I am wouldn't
forever be a person misread

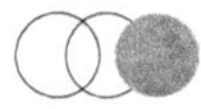

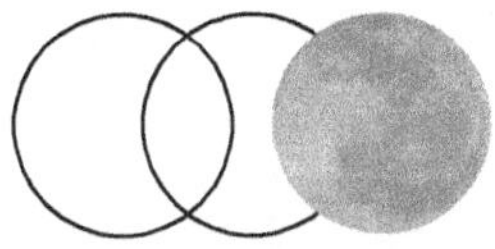

Chapter III:
Erasures

Where You Had Me Left

My words form into poetry,
as I am there describing every
feeling and situation

Yet thinking about you
has me speechless,
and for that I have no
valid explanation

Months later and still,
I am there where you had me left

Far away you have fled,
not held accountable for a heart-theft

Wishes of a soulmate,
will always have your name

And what we once shared,
I'll try as hard to reclaim

Words, poetry, and lyrics
would fall short, describing
how your aura ignited a glow
so incandescent

...

Immortalized is the love I have
for you, in the darkest nights,
you're a breathtaking crescent

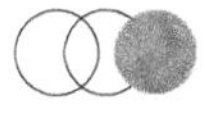

Favorable Outcomes

Despite the rarity of
favorable outcomes,
two of my friends have shared
a birthday with you

A sign, I believed it was,
forming an instant attachment
that I hadn't thought through

Our moons each other overlap
and complete, and our stars
do perfectly align

My soulmate I'd swear you are,
bound we were to cross paths
by sweet divine

Never felt satisfaction with
a person's existence, as much
I did with yours

Only my own company I used to enjoy,
until your aura fragranced its lures

...

Made a fool of myself,
with delusion I have did

Nonexistent I was,
on your meticulous life grid

Yet, months pass by,
and from the haunted restaurant
I never get to leave

Every August, pain resurfaces,
a potential of an enormous bond
I get to grieve

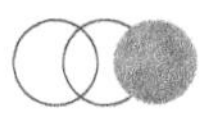

I Still You See

Six months later,
and no matter how hard I try,
about you I cannot stop thinking

The grudge of knowing you
is enough, to stop the bones
you broke from mending

Maybe if you have bothered,
or have even given it an ounce
of thought

Haunted I wouldn't be,
rowing by your careless words
on a wrecked boat

All alone I am now,
after you have fled and
supposedly set me free

Yet my mind is jailed
by memories of you,
in everything I still you see

. . .

Erasures of you is something I now
desperately implore

To close off doors of trauma that
shook me to the core

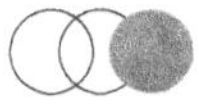

Erasures

Recalling previous
conversations, now I do

My sight overtaken,
by pigments of no hue

A trajectory I never wished
for us to witness

Yet it's a life regular,
ensuing with swiftness

No matter the preserving,
it always slips through

Pure luminescence dimmed,
and itself withdrew

Phasing from a crescent,
to a gibbous, to a full moon

And to a darkened new moon,
that would us maroon

...

A way out of it,
you ultimately find,
but I am still here

My cries flood a village,
while you barely shed a tear

No matter the grieving,
moving on feels so extreme

And memory erasures,
only exist in a perfect dream

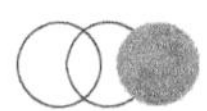

Lovesick

Don't you think it's a shame how my
heart pumps with rhythms of your name?

How it does not seem to yet realize
that about me you couldn't less care?

A distant dream you grow to be,
and I see it slipping through my
fingers

Midst whispered sighs I feel it,
an ultimate failure of a potential
lingers

With every heartbeat,
loud echoes of your essence pulse
a haunting refrain

Treacherous is the unrequitedness,
longing I am for a remedy to such pain

...

A wandering lone sailor I am,
navigating through endless volumes
of my despair

A festering emptiness within me
sprouts, a sense of feeling I can
no longer bear

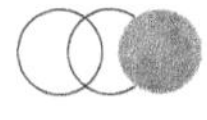

Hyper Independence

No longer bound I am,
by the constraints of a passion
that has faltered and fell

With a newfound clarity,
I walk this trail alone, and on
delusions I no longer dwell

Hyper independence I now reclaim,
as the last I'll write about you
these words will be

Soulmates we supposedly were,
and it once cut deep not surviving
through destiny

Similar our defining characters
are, and pushing us apart that
ultimately did

Identical puzzle pieces we stood,
and exact magnet poles that synergy
do forbid

...

Saddening of a truth it is,
and the one person I truly loved
has gripped on hyper independence

A personality trait I still own,
yet I gracefully had it suppressed
when I had you in attendance

All the same are our favorite movies,
our comfort tasks and hobbies, our
coinciding music taste

Yet it's time to go, even as I have
seen through you schemes of colors
that are never to be replaced

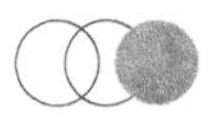

43

Chapter IV:
Eclipses

AHMED ABOELHIBA

Duplicity

Insane, how my character holds a
mirror to those whom I once loved

How absorbing actions and preferences
of theirs is on me behoved

Deranged, how through morning mirrors
I see myself as a tapestry of people
I have once knew

Clothing style, music taste, and even
quite an uncanny resemblance that has
eventually grew

Insensible, how within miracle
personality-studios,
I spend hours and years crafting
changeable identities

An "odd man out" evens out
the quirks and oddities,
reshaping dreams of sweet
company into realities

...

Mindless, how my mind works endless
efforts of temporary results of great
appeal and character

How it aims to unrecall those who
almost shed me apart, yet sticking
around is their eternal spectre

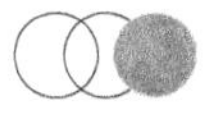

Passenger Seat

Here we go again,
another dream left untouched
within the drafts of life

A passion left unspoken of,
a promising career cut through
with the sharpest knife

The lives we're born into, are known
to be as scarce and precious as gold

Yet, of our lives we usually get the
passenger seat, and asking for full
control might be a request too bold

A realization then hits if there
has ever been any sort of choice

Not every action we are granted,
and we merely stand as observing
reactions with a muted voice

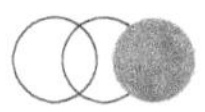

Moved On

I told myself I moved on,
but I don't think it was ever true

A failure of a mind-trick,
turning my best of days to blue

I told myself I grew out of love,
but the ache of longing keeps
festering

Triggered I am by any reminder,
and myself I am currently sequestering

I told myself closure is in distance,
but I whispered lies to mask the pain

Always seen I am wearing smiles,
yet in solitude, tears stream
like rain

. . .

I told myself I'd erase each memory,
but these stubborn stains are refusing
to fade

Like etchings on glass, they remain;
those flashbacks sound a taunting
serenade

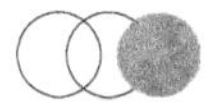

Calendar Days

Countless days lapse through my
calendar drifting aimlessly by,

Each one sounds a silent echo,
without a tear or even a sigh

Yet in the quiet corners of my mind,
a thought rises and takes flight,

Could one of these forgotten days
find its moment to shine in light?

An anniversary,
or a friend's birthday perhaps

Or even a lovely evening
of wholesome recaps

These anchors of days,
they keep me going,
they keep me alive,

In their anticipation,
I find something to live for,
I find the strength to thrive

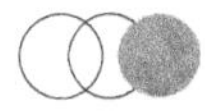

Venice

Oh how often does my mind keep
reminding me of my trip to Venice,

How joy gushed through my nerves,
how time never felt more precious

How often does my mind keep
digging up agonies of the anchor
keychain I've back then bought

How a souvenir to my grandmother
it was, how she couldn't have it
before she'd to heaven teleport

How often do I realize
it was supposed to remind her of me,
how it was a supposed lovely gift

How it is now one thing I have from
her, how it is something she hadn't
even known did exist

...

How often does the anchor keychain
anchor me down, even when it is still
in gift paper wrapped

How a tiny souvenir from Venice has
caught lots of feelings, leaving them
bottled up and trapped

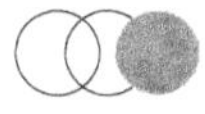

Gabriel

Through the night, in a dream,
visits a little boy named Gabriel

A guy with smart intuition,
with one glance you can tell

Conversations take us by,
and in blinks of an eye into another
person he grows up too fast

A precocious young man he is now,
and for some reason I'm aware of
memories of his past

Unlike the others,
materialism means nothing to
the pure soul he encompasses

Like any other,
he dreams of company that chooses
him apart from the masses

. . .

Walking down fake streets of mind,
Gabriel tells me he wishes to find
someone who'd see into him

Who'd flesh out his good
and appreciate his flaws,
away from brutal contempt
or sorts of whim

Mirrors of myself I see through that
kid, and I assure him the universe
shall align to his favor

He waves me goodbye as the dream calls
off, and into his world he steps in as
someone braver

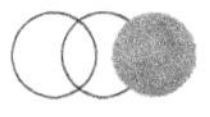

55

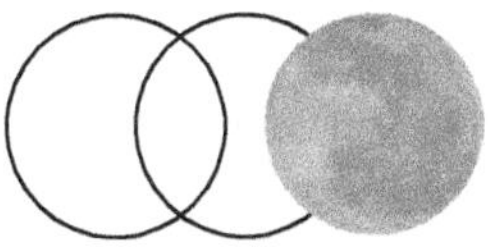

Chapter V:
Tapestry

Tapestry

Your presence around me was a true
shift from shades of grayscale to
screaming color

Harsh winters changing to lively
springs, a desert remolding into
a forest like no other

Our deep conversations were puzzle
boards in no time complete

Igniting incandescence,
the enormous shine of a
crescent so elite

Your inevitable contempt fated
blooming roses to die and wilt

Overflowed a jug begging for no more,
and has all over spilt

. . .

Your non-explanatory behavior left
a mesmerizing poem with no ending

Blinded eyes off a starry night,
had thrill ride queues forever
extending

Your leave of me shred
a vintage tapestry apart

Shattered vases of glass,
ruined symbolic art

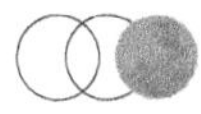

Way Kinder

Not even second-best I am to them,
despite my maximum efforts to have
them around

Drifting away they are,
from a mountain top they push me
down to the coldest ground

And nothing explains
why they would act as such

Reasons to hate me?
I don't think there are much

Their attitude shifts,
and for some reason they are
now way kinder

To someone they disregarded,
and maybe their guilt serves
a reminder

...

And I get to see glimpses
of how our conversations have shaped

The strong bond, we would have
long ago formed and sustained

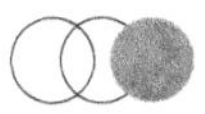

Watch

A watch I used to wear
every day on my wrist

Yet the idea of having one,
you used to resist

Caused discomfort to you, it did,
and like a handcuff it felt

Intriguing to me, that was,
and a thought I haven't with
momentarily dealt

And as the clock ticks,
out of my watches I have now grown

And why you disliked them,
I've finally understood and known

Would've never expected,
that you would now watches wear

As clear as day,
of how we both changed,
I'm now well aware

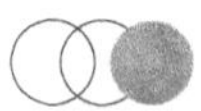

Relentless Chattering

Away they have drifted and fled,
yet acceptant I am, and I could not
anymore care

Niceness I still offer, the checking
up I still do, willingly, as I am not
a circus glare

Trigger their anger their broken ego
will do, and more hatred for me will
their heart consume

With it they even realize,
how throwing me away will
eventually their life gloom

Enough evidence I am from them piling,
and all the receipts I am meticulously
gathering

Their guilt-tripping no more
functions,
their victim-playing sounds
like relentless chattering

. . .

Like a diamond they are,
its shine seems so blinding
and fluorescent

Yet it a fake it is,
and within worthless competitions
they are always present

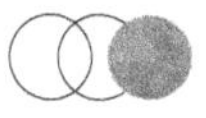

Ruins

Is it my fault that you
ruin everything?
Am I to blame for your words
that sting?

Why did all the talks turn
into festering silence?
Is it because to your suppression
I paid no compliance?

The spark of your presence,
have previously pumped into
my heart reviving blood

Now through my veins runs
deep-blue ink, shaping words
that into paper thud

And I couldn't help but wonder,
if you have found it too easy
to part ways

To call someone close a stranger,
brushing off the sweetest of days

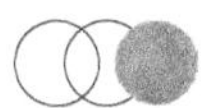

As If

You doubt that I am smart,
as if falsifying a fact would
change what I already know

"I'll give you that," you say,
as if you expect that I would
for you now kneel and bow

Words of yours mark signals,
weighted with loads of hatred
and layers of disdain

Your egoistic sense of superiority
drips from you, like endless showers
of acid rain

You tell me I am brave,
as if my courage is something
you have paved

"I'll give you that," you mutter,
as if my spirit is something you
have enslaved

. . .

Yet, not defined I am
by your arrogant, skewed perception

Nor am I ever bound
by your pretentious, biased conception

Share your thoughts if you must;
your words are mere strokes upon
my sacred canvas

Shaping my own image I am,
and I handpick my hues all the way
from Cairo to Kansas

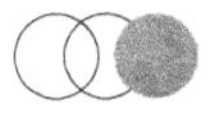

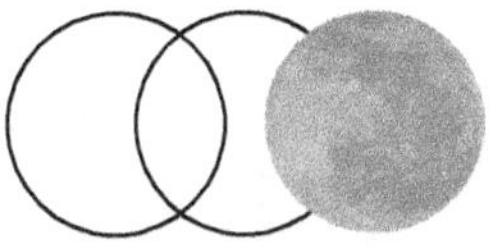

Chapter VI:
Telescopic

No Longer Twenty-One

No longer twenty-one,
he realizes he now is

Over now is an age,
that gave him enormous bliss

No longer twenty-one he is,
speed-running through what is
ahead of years

Drained of energy he is,
and between the crowds he fades
and disappears

No longer twenty-one he is,
and age is no more a milestone
to celebrate

All the lyrics describing
23's and 25's,
make the joy within him
dissipate

...

No longer twenty-one he is,
and into a changed person
he eventually grew

And he longs to a version of himself,
that have mirrored a more uplifting
view

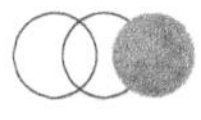

Felicity

One day, our lives into one
another intertwine and converge

One another we get to know,
a chemistry sprouts and emerges

Sweet acquaintances,
to lovely coworkers, to close friends

An overload of felicity sprouting
from their presence eventually ends

As time and its passage does not
always allow for a forever

Yet these moments and memories,
we still cherish whatsoever

One day, paths diverge,
and us all together,
in pictures we can only see

Still counting on the day,
where we're served to a reunion,
by some decree

Reflection

They probably don't know this,
but I just think of them always

Whenever I spot something that
they adore or constantly praise

A true reflection of them,
I see in what they love

A reflection of what they love,
I see in them too

And as we grow older,
each other we don't get to encounter
for many months and days

Yet they will always be present,
with the spirit of what I associate
with them anyways

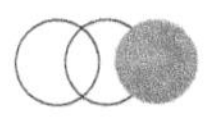

Outsider

What he wants he always seems to get,
an outsider would bet

Not what he needs though,
and to failure he is constantly set

No matter how long he is leading,
he ends up second-best after a minor
stumble

Engraved in memory these are,
experiences that will never fail
to him humble

Finding a soulmate bloomed him up,
as it was on the verge of happening

Yet never-lasting that was,
and what was fun ended up
his life blackening

...

An outsider he is around everyone,
and in every place he finds himself
present

Only finding company as he gazes
up the skies, spotting clouds and
crescents

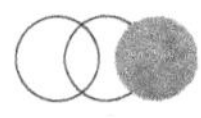

Tomorrow's Memories

Consuming his visions are immense
doses of tomorrow's memories

Blurring his thinking it is,
yet he is in no need of mental
remedies

Tomorrow's memories were once
an overwhelming past's future

Between both he exists, and the
wound of time he tries to suture

An iridescence of possibilities
ahead of him, with much patience
and caution he awaits

His unsure footsteps mark a trail,
yet an alignment with tomorrow's
memories it dictates

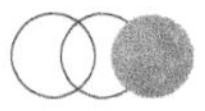

Pull Up Stakes

The limitless academic expectations
by others set,
The pressure of the grades he tries
as hard to get

The trauma of undesired grades,
not being good enough
The burnouts he best avoids
when times get tough

Sleepless nights,
endless dedication,
tired eyes

Stepping stones they are,
ones he needs to rise

The great friends he makes,
the new experiences he commits to
and easily overtakes

A transforming journey it was,
with much confidence he is now
ready to pull up stakes

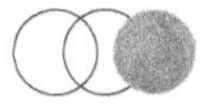

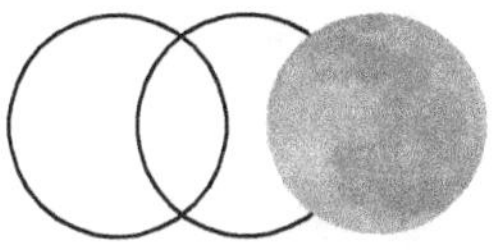

Chapter VII:
Chemistry

Chemistry

Blind her eyes were,
and beyond aristocracy
she can barely see

Blind her eyes are,
and to see that figure far away
she can only plea

Blind his eyes were,
by dreams of a life that has
ever been robbed from him

Yet resolute he is,
striving to escape the darkened
tunnel, one so dim

And it wasn't until they met
where the blindness truly unfolded

A spark of electrifying chemistry
had a sense of eternity molded

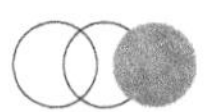

Figments

The type of person he is,
beautifully appearing

Through glimpses of dreams,
she wakes up joy-tearing

Realization then hits,
too ideal to be true,
this person is

"Another figments of imagination,"
her mind just says

Yet here he does exist;
figments creep and into
reality manifest

And so their love exists;
its presence has them both
deeply blessed

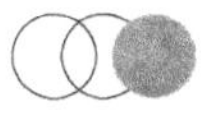

Mahogany

Robber of her cure he initially was,
until he aimed for her heart instead

And across her manor,
a so-called butler had
his piano notes spread

The gentle gestures,
the intimate whispers

The aftermath of a gun
aimed at a forehead;
the consolation she felt
as he kissed hers

And as the clock ticks,
different ways they have
eventually parted

Yet he'll always be there,
from her mind he never departed

Living, Breathing Art

Cloud patterns, crescent sky
Perfections one cannot stage or buy

Gazing through her eyes,
the heavens in awe sigh

Mountains collapse and bow,
rivers pause and shy

As she talks,
her chords echo symphonies of spring

Like whispering winds,
an elite charm it does bring

As bright as moonlight,
is her presence

Unlike any other,
a bewitching luminescence

...

Yet she doesn't seem to realize,
that within her, all elements
conspire and rhyme

Her character mirrors a reflection,
of fine melodies, woven through space
and time

And the cosmos couldn't help but find
in her its truest form of art

Her aura spellbinds, akin to how stars
through the night skies chart

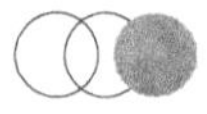

Winters to Spring

A long lost gem she has in him found

Took her long enough,
but she's finally here with him around

And the people before him,
exhausted her and had the light
within her dimmed

Turned her colors to grayscale,
and blew off her feathers by
a severe wind

In prayers she hopes she never loses
him, even knowing forever was never
a real thing

And she hopes he does see in her too,
someone who would change his winters
to spring

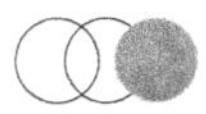

And He Told Her

Pupils of hers were of no sight,
yet he remained her fluorescent
beaming light

Through halls of echoing whispers
and murmurs of night,
he guided her steps, kept her path
always safe and bright

"Exactly," and he told her,
"the world is a song, each note a
direction, one you knew all along."

Down staircases she went cautiously,
sensing her lefts and rights,
following trails of symphonic winds,
moving along as airy kites

Underneath starry heavens of night,
he told her stories, and made her
soul take flight

"Exactly," and he told her,
"these stars are mirrors of your
spirit, ones where your true vision
is from, inherent."

...

Where shadows screened
nature's delight,
he painted her in colors,
her heart's own respite

And together they wandered,
through life's endless maze,
her sightless eyes brightened,
by an igniting cerulean haze

"Exactly," and he told her,
"you see through your heart, no
blindness can sever a true bond
apart."

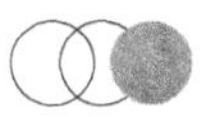

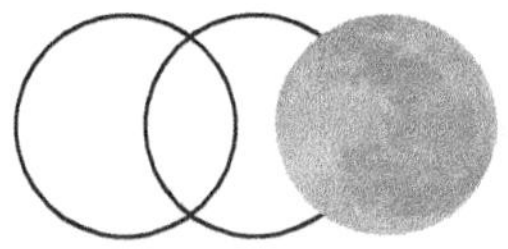

Chapter VIII:
Cerulean

Within

Within miseries,
you would find me making larks,
because I always win

No matter what happens, it must be
for the good, I say with a wide grin

Within breakdowns,
you would find me writing, because
pain can never have on me a lead

I turn them into words of poetry, and
what once broke me down is now having
me succeed

Within despair,
I am always in lands of fiction,
because reveries can lift the heaviest
of hearts

Fragments of my dreaming weave into
reality, and the festering chaos away
from me departs

...

Within ruins,
you would see in me an architect,
because rubbles can rise into what
is grand

I gather the pieces and together
they do culminate, and I create
colossal castles from the sand

Within storms,
you would find in me a voyager,
because tempests test the best
sailors' skills

I navigate endless seas of burden
tenaciously, and I aim for serenity
within the wildest thrills

Within farewells,
you would find me content, because
each goodbye declares a new start

I embrace the journey with whatever
it beholds, and incandescence ignites
within my heart

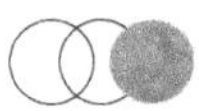

November 16

Every night, back to November 16,
my mind keeps taking me

An anniversary of a book that from
agony has set me free

Words took shape into a sweet
antidote, wiping away all the
heaviness accumulating

And to the kaleidoscope of feelings
and experiences, I found myself
heavily relating

Eventually such a creation has evolved
into an inseparable companion of mine

A go-to for consolation and ultimate
relief, a book shaped by exquisite
design

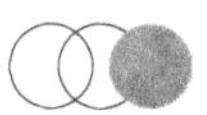

The Person He Is

An elite academic achiever,
an ultimate people pleaser

Thoughtful and smart,
a person with outgoing demeanor

By others' presence around him,
he finds himself experiencing pure joy

All the laughs and talks vanish away
his deep-rooted pain and destroy

Despite the constant struggles,
the in-mind battles

Staying strong he is,
he does not feel at all rattled

A firm believer he is,
that someday he will find
what he deeply deserves

Appreciation for the person he is,
without any doubts or reserves

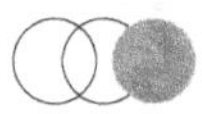

Sunshine

Golden, shining as the
brightest star out there

Incandescent, your soul and presence
are, and nothing else can compare

Thoughtful you are, about
conversations we together shared

With every tiny specificity and
detail, in your mind engraved

Anxious I am, one day I will you lose
No other gal I can instead choose

Sunshine you are,
a ray of light in a darkened room

With every lighthearted joke
and sagacious advice, making
wilted souls once again bloom

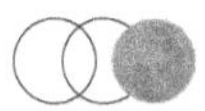

Take Me Back

Take me back,
through flashbacks of time

To the moment we've met,
one so sublime

Take me back,
to the relentless planning
to achieve goals in mind

Despite the worrying and anxiety,
it has the best of times defined

Take me back.
to having a smaller circle
of understanding friends

As its expansion had some walking out,
leaving behind loose ends

...

Take me back, yet keep me here,
as I do not wish to be again blinded

By false expectations,
that had me through life lost
and misguided

Keep me here,
as it's where I now
reside and belong

And there's no true fun,
in a never-ending song

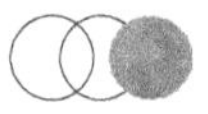

Good Riddance

Much pain at first,
good riddance at last

Our lives move on,
with characters recast

Schedules rearrange,
lists refine

Meticulous days,
we opt to design

From habits of affection,
good riddance at last

Our view of life changes,
with vivid contrast

Eyes wandering in awe,
within cerulean skies

Carefree states of mind,
that do not surmise

...

Self-scrutiny we abandon;
good riddance at last

Spells that once haunted us,
are no longer cast

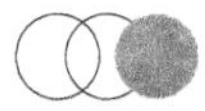

The Epilogue

AHMED ABOELHIBA

We Are Merely A Kaleidoscope

Sometimes, the hardships of the present makes you deeply reminisce on the sweetness of the past. In many other times, the satisfying present could have never been possible without the hardships of the past. Regardless though, we are merely a kaleidoscope of experiences and memories, interactions and relationships, as well as successes and challenges, and that is what the core of Cerulean is truly about.

You look at the cerulean sky and gaze into its mesmerizing aura, but has it always been in such a state? Definitely not. Day changes to night, cerulean changes to purple-pink to black, sun changes to moon, and even the moon itself phases and changes throughout.

Humans do phase too. From a new moon, to a crescent, a quarter, a gibbous, and to a full moon. It is a never-ending cycle.

Whether knowingly or not, we experience the phasing of our personalities and characters as we grow, by every single situation we are living through and by the memory banks we keep reflecting and reminiscing upon.

Through every circumstance, we are eventually lead to countless lifelong realizations on who we are and where we stand within this ever-expanding world.